Heavenly Homemaker's

SIMPLE
REAL FOOD
RECIPES

Laura Coppinger

A NOTE FROM LAURA –

I considered dedicating Simple Real Food Recipes to my Crock Pot, but I didn't want my Instant Pot to feel left out. Both are unwavering MVPs of my kitchen.

But I'd be nowhere without my family – my willing taste testers and the best reasons I constantly need to look for ways to create Simple Real Food Recipes. Keeping up with my large tribe of men is my absolute joy, and staying ahead of them in the kitchen is my favorite challenge.

This is all well and good, but if you asked me how Simple Real Food Recipes *really* came to be, I'd have to say this: God did it.

Well, of course He did.

I mean, giving credit to God is a must with anything we do. But truly, when I look back at the past three years at all God has been doing in my life I can see that He long ago began preparing me in the kitchen for the surprise turn of events He was about to reveal.

You see, I used to think I was busy, because I was. Busy. A husband, four sons, a thriving blog, several beautiful ministries in our community – I was busy.

Therefore I had the idea to start using real food ingredients to make the simplest recipes I could. Why make healthy eating complicated, right? We want to eat well, but we're all busy, right? Everyone can use recipes like this! So I started to create.

Simple Real Food Recipe ideas kept coming, and they turned into this book.

Three years after my original idea, I look back and see the real reason God started this project. He'd been planning all along to add to our family. Surprised? I sure was. Four boys turned into five, thanks to the gift and challenge of foster care and adoption. And now there are two other Bonus Babes in our care. Who else will He add? Only God knows.

What would I do during this season in our lives without Simple Real Food Recipes? Phew. I don't want to know. But I do know that these recipes and this book show that God works out every detail as He prepares us to take part in His perfect plans for each of us – even so much as teaching me how to throw dry pasta into a crock pot with some sauce so I could let my family's dinner cook itself while I rock babies and keep up with my teenagers too.

So this book is for you and for me – all who are striving to feed our families well while we spend more time focused on all that really matters in this life: God and His people.

The recipes are simple, made from real food, and will take you very little time or effort to prepare. As an added bonus, we think they all taste great!

Plus, we'd love for you to join us regularly at our online community: HeavenlyHomemakers.com. We share real food, real family, and real life. Come be a part – the Simple Real Food Recipe ideas keep coming!

TABLE OF CONTENTS

SIMPLE INSTANT POT RECIPES

SIMPLE SNACKS & DESSERTS

SIMPLE SOUPS

SIMPLE CROCK POT CHICKEN SOUP WITH A KICK

Serves: 4-6

Ingredients

- 2 pounds boneless chicken thighs or breasts

- 16 ounces salsa (more or less is fine)

- 32 ounces (1 quart) chicken broth

- 8 ounces cheese (cheddar, Colby jack, Monterrey, Pepper jack - whichever you prefer)

Instructions

1. Put all ingredients into a crock pot.

2. Cook on hi for 3-4 hours or low for 6-8.

3. Shred chicken and serve.

20 MINUTE TACO SOUP

Serves: 4-6

Ingredients

- 1 pound ground beef

- 16 ounces salsa (more or less is fine; mild to hot is fine - your preference)

- 32 ounces (1 quart) chicken or beef broth

- 8 ounces cheese (Colby jack or cheddar)

Instructions

1. In a medium to large sized pot, brown the hamburger meat until no longer pink.

2. Stir in salsa and broth and heat with the meat.

3. Cut cheese into small chunks and stir into the soup, whisking until melted.

Top with your favorite taco ingredients!
- Crushed tortilla chips
- Sour Cream
- Sliced Olives
- Black Beans
- Corn

SIMPLE HAMBURGER SOUP

Serves: 4-6

Ingredients

- 1 pound hamburger

- 3 Tablespoons minced onion

- 2-3 cups frozen green beans

- 2-3 cups frozen corn (optional)

- 32 ounces tomato soup

- Sea salt to taste

- 1 cup shredded Colby jack or cheddar cheese

Instructions

1. Brown hamburger and minced onion until meat is no longer pink.

2. Meanwhile, steam green beans in a separate pot until they are tender.

3. Stir together cooked meat mixture, green beans, corn, and tomato soup.

4. Simmer until bubbly, salting liberally.

5. Serve in bowls with shredded cheese if desired.

SIMPLE NOODLE SOUP

Serves: 4-6

Ingredients

- 4 cups of your favorite broth
- 2-3 carrots
- 1½ cups of your favorite whole grain pasta, any shape or variety
- Sea salt and pepper to taste
- Additional veggies your family likes in soup

Instructions

1. Pour broth into a large cooking pot.
2. Slice carrots (and other veggies if you like) and add to the pot.
3. Bring broth and carrots to a boil.
4. Add pasta, salt, and pepper.
5. Cook until pasta is tender, about 8 minutes.

SIMPLE

EVERY DAY

RECIPES

SIMPLE BAKED SALMON AND ASPARAGUS

Serves: 4-6 | Oven: 400°

Ingredients

- 4-5 salmon fillets

- 1 pound (give or take) fresh asparagus

- 2 Tablespoons olive oil

- 2 Tablespoons lemon juice

- Sea salt and pepper to taste

- 1 medium onion

Instructions

1. Lay asparagus along the bottom of a 9x13 inch baking dish.

2. Place salmon fillets over the asparagus.

3. Drizzle olive oil and lemon juice over salmon and asparagus, then sprinkle with salt and pepper.

4. Slice onion, then lay the slices over the salmon.

5. Cover and bake in a 400° oven for 20 minutes.

SIMPLE SKILLET TACO PASTA

Serves: 4-6

Ingredients

- 1 pound hamburger meat

- Sea salt and pepper to taste

- 1 teaspoon chili powder

- ½ teaspoon garlic powder

- 16 ounces salsa

- 1½ cups water

- 8 ounces whole grain pasta, any shape (gluten free works great too!)

- 8 ounces shredded cheddar or Colby jack cheese

Instructions

1. In a large skillet, brown hamburger meat until no longer pink.

2. Drain excess grease if necessary.

3. Season meat with salt, pepper, chili powder, and garlic powder.

4. Stir in salsa, water, and pasta. Bring to a boil.

5. Turn down heat to simmer, cover and cook for about 10 minutes or until pasta is tender.

6. Turn off heat, sprinkle cheese over the mixture in the skillet, and put the lid on for 2 minutes to melt the cheese.

SIMPLE CRUNCHY RANCH CHICKEN STRIPS

Serves: 4-6 | Oven: 375°

Ingredients

- 2 pounds boneless chicken breasts
- ½ cup grated parmesan cheese
- ½ cup whole grain flour (rice, wheat, corn, etc) or crushed corn flakes
- 3 Tablespoons Ranch Dressing Mix*
- 1 cup melted butter, divided

Instructions

1. Cut chicken into strips about 1 inch wide.

2. Drizzle ½ cup melted butter into the bottom of a 9x13 inch baking dish.

3. In a bowl, stir together parmesan cheese, flour, and ranch dressing mix.

4. Stir in the chicken pieces until they are coated.

5. Spread the prepared chicken pieces into the butter in the pan.

6. Drizzle the remaining butter over the chicken.

7. Bake in a 375° oven for 25 minutes or until chicken is no longer pink.

8. If desired, broil chicken for about 2 minutes to crisp it up before serving.

*Ranch Seasoning

Ingredients

- 5 Tablespoons dried minced onions
- 7 teaspoons parsley flakes
- 4 teaspoons sea salt
- 1 teaspoon garlic powder

Instructions

- Mix together and store in an air tight container.
- For dressing: Mix 2 Tablespoons dry mix with 1 cup mayonnaise and 1 cup buttermilk or sour cream.
- For dip: Mix 2 Tablespoons dry mix with 2 cups sour cream or Creme Fraiche.
- Mix up a few hours before serving, so the flavors all blend nicely.

SIMPLE HONEY MUSTARD CHICKEN LEGS

Serves: 4-6 | Oven: 350°

Ingredients

- 2 pounds (give or take) chicken legs (or any variety of chicken pieces you like)
- 3 Tablespoons mustard
- 2-3 teaspoons honey
- ¼ teaspoon garlic powder
- ¼ teaspoon sea salt

Instructions

1. Place chicken pieces in a 9x13 inch baking dish.
2. Mix remaining ingredients in a bowl and spread over the top of the chicken.
3. Bake uncovered in a 350° oven for 50-60 minutes or until chicken is golden brown and juices run clear.

SIMPLE SWEET AND SOUR BAKED CHICKEN LEGS

Serves: 4-6 | Oven: 350°

Ingredients

- 2 pounds chicken legs (other pieces work fine too but may require more baking time)

- 2 Tablespoons honey

- ¼ cup soy sauce

- ½ cup ketchup

- 3 cloves garlic

- Sea salt and pepper to taste

Instructions

1. Lay chicken legs in a 9x13 inch baking dish.

2. Mix honey, soy sauce, ketchup, and garlic in a small saucepan. Heat briefly to melt honey and to make sure ingredients are well combined.

3. Spread mixture over chicken legs.

4. Cover and bake in a 350°oven for 45 minutes. Turn chicken over in the sauce, cover, and cook for 15 minutes more.

BE SURE
THE SOY SAUCE
IS GLUTEN FREE
IF THIS IS A NEED
FOR YOU !

SIMPLE ITALIAN BEEF AND BROCCOLI SKILLET

Serves: 4-6

Ingredients

- 1-2 pounds beef stew meat

- 3 Tablespoons dry Italian seasoning mix*

- 1 medium head fresh broccoli

- 2 Tablespoons olive oil

Instructions

1. Stir ingredients together in a skillet.

2. Cover and let meat cook on low heat for about 45 minutes to 1 hour, stirring occasionally.

3. Serve with rice if you like.

*Italian Dressing Mix

Ingredients

- 1½ teaspoons garlic powder

- 1 Tablespoon onion powder

- 2 teaspoons oregano

- 1 Tablespoon dried parsley

- 2 teaspoons sea salt

- 1 teaspoon pepper

- ¼ teaspoon thyme

- ½ teaspoon dried celery flakes

Instructions

Shake ingredients together and store in a jar.

To make Italian salad dressing: Mix 2 Tablespoons dry mix with ¼ cup vinegar (I prefer red wine vinegar), 2 teaspoons water and ½ cup olive oil.

SIMPLE TACO RICE DINNER

Serves: 4-6

Ingredients

- 1 cup brown rice

- 1 pound ground beef

- 1 teaspoon chili powder

- ½ teaspoon garlic powder

- Sea salt to taste

- 15 ounces (give or take) salsa

- 15 ounces cooked black beans

- 1-2 cups shredded cheddar or Colby jack cheese

Instructions

1. Boil two cups of water, add rice, turn down to very low heat, cover, and simmer for 45 minutes until rice is cooked.

2. In the meantime, brown ground beef in a separate skillet until no longer pink.

3. Add chili powder, garlic powder, and salt.

4. Stir together cooked rice, cooked meat, salsa, and black beans.

5. Serve as-is if you need to avoid dairy. Or sprinkle cheese on top and serve!

SIMPLE LAST-MINUTE NACHO PLATE

Serves: 4-6

Ingredients

- 1½ pounds ground beef

- 15 ounces salsa

- 1 cup shredded cheese

- Tortilla chips and your favorite nacho fixin's

Instructions

1. Brown hamburger meat until it is no longer pink.

2. Stir in salsa and cheese.

3. Serve on a plate of tortilla chips with your favorite nacho fixin's.

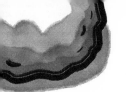

SIMPLE CHICKEN CHEESEBALLS WITH A KICK

Serves: 6-8 servings | Oven: 350°

Ingredients

- 2 pounds ground chicken
- 4 cups shredded cheddar or Colby jack cheese
- 1½ teaspoons onion powder
- 1 teaspoon garlic powder
- ½ teaspoon sea salt
- 2 Tablespoons hot sauce (I use Cholula)

Instructions

1. Mix all ingredients together in a bowl until well combined.

2. Scoop mixture into 1" balls into a 9x13 inch baking dish.

3. Bake in a 350° oven for 20-25 minutes or until balls are nice and brown.

4. Pour off excess grease that has accumulated before serving.

SIMPLE PIZZA CHICKEN BAKE

Serves: 4-6 | Oven: 400°

Ingredients

- 3 pounds boneless chicken breasts or thighs

- 14 ounces pizza sauce

- 2 cups shredded mozzarella cheese

- 6 ounces sliced pepperoni

Instructions

1. Cut chicken into thin strips and spread them into the bottom of a 9x13 inch baking dish.

2. Spread pizza sauce over the chicken.

3. Sprinkle with cheese.

4. Top with pepperoni.

5. Bake uncovered in a 400° oven for 30 minutes or until chicken is no longer pink.

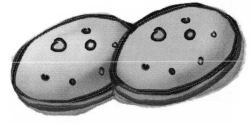

SIMPLE 5-MINUTE ITALIAN CHICKEN BAKE

Serves: 4-6 | Oven: 400°

Ingredients

- 1-2 pounds boneless chicken thighs or breasts

- 2-3 cups frozen green beans

- 1 cup Italian dressing*

Instructions

1. Lay chicken in a 9x13 baking dish.

2. Pour green beans over the chicken.

3. Pour Italian dressing over the beans and chicken.

4. Cover and bake in a 400° oven for 45 minutes to 1 hour or until chicken is no longer pink.

*Italian Dressing Mix

Ingredients

- 1½ teaspoons garlic powder

- 1 Tablespoon onion powder

- 2 teaspoons oregano

- 1 Tablespoon dried parsley

- 2 teaspoons sea salt

- 1 teaspoon pepper

- ¼ teaspoon thyme

- ½ teaspoon dried celery flakes

Instructions

Shake ingredients together and store in a jar.

To make Italian salad dressing: Mix 2 Tablespoons dry mix with ¼ cup vinegar (I prefer red wine vinegar), 2 teaspoons water and ½ cup olive oil.

SIMPLE BACON RANCH CHICKEN

Serves: 4-6 | Oven: 350°

Ingredients

- 4-6 chicken boneless breasts or thighs

- ½ pound bacon

- ½ cup ranch dressing*

- 1 cup shredded cheddar or Colby jack cheese

Instructions

1. Lay chicken pieces in the bottom of a 9x13 inch baking dish.

2. Spread ranch dressing over the chicken.

3. Lay strips of uncooked bacon over the ranch-covered chicken.

4. Sprinkle cheese over the top.

5. Bake uncovered, in a 350° oven for 25-45 minutes or until chicken is no longer pink.

*Ranch Seasoning

Ingredients

- 5 Tablespoons dried minced onions

- 7 teaspoons parsley flakes

- 4 teaspoons sea salt

- 1 teaspoon garlic powder

Instructions

- Mix together and store in an air tight container.

- For dressing: Mix 2 Tablespoons dry mix with 1 cup mayonnaise and 1 cup buttermilk or sour cream.

- For dip: Mix 2 Tablespoons dry mix with 2 cups sour cream or Creme Fraiche.

- Mix up a few hours before serving, so the flavors all blend nicely.

SIMPLE GARLIC BUTTER SHRIMP

Serves: 3-5

Ingredients

- 2 pounds raw shrimp (any size, frozen or thawed)

- ¼-½ cup butter

- 2 teaspoons garlic powder or freshly minced garlic

Instructions

1. Cook ingredients together in a skillet for 20-30 minutes, stirring occasionally.

2. Easy as that!

SIMPLE 5-MINUTE ITALIAN CHICKEN BAKE

Serves: 4-6 | Oven: 400°

Ingredients

- 1-2 pounds boneless chicken thighs or breasts

- 2-3 cups frozen green beans

- 1 cup Italian dressing*

Instructions

1. Lay chicken in a 9x13 baking dish.

2. Pour green beans over the chicken.

3. Pour Italian dressing over the beans and chicken.

4. Cover and bake in a 400° oven for 45 minutes to 1 hour or until chicken is no longer pink.

*Italian Dressing Mix

Ingredients

- 1½ teaspoons garlic powder

- 1 Tablespoon onion powder

- 2 teaspoons oregano

- 1 Tablespoon dried parsley

- 2 teaspoons sea salt

- 1 teaspoon pepper

- ¼ teaspoon thyme

- ½ teaspoon dried celery flakes

Instructions

Shake ingredients together and store in a jar.

To make Italian salad dressing: Mix 2 Tablespoons dry mix with ¼ cup vinegar (I prefer red wine vinegar), 2 teaspoons water and ½ cup olive oil.

SIMPLE CHEESE-STUFFED BURGERS

Serves: 6-8

Ingredients

- 2 pounds hamburger meat

- 8 ounces cream cheese (or any cheese you like)

- Sea salt and pepper to taste

Instructions

1. Divide meat into 8 patties.

2. Cut cheese into 8 pieces.

3. Wrap meat around the cheese and flatten slightly.

4. Grill or pan fry until meat is no longer pink, seasoning to your liking.

5. Serve right away.

SIMPLE LENTIL NACHOS

Serves: 6-8

Ingredients

- 1 cup dry lentils

- 2½ cups water

- 16 ounces salsa

- Your favorite nacho toppings like cheese, olives, peppers, lettuce, tomatoes, guacamole, and onions

- Your favorite tortilla chips

Instructions

1. In a medium-sized saucepan, stir together lentils and water.

2. Bring to a boil.

3. Reduce heat and simmer for 15-20 minutes or until lentils are tender.

4. Stir in salsa, heating for an additional 2 minutes.

5. Serve mixture with tortilla chips and your favorite nacho toppings

THE EASIEST WAY TO MAKE LASAGNA

Serves: 6-10 | Oven: 350°

Ingredients

- 1 pound ground hamburger meat

- 4 Tablespoons minced onion or chopped fresh onion

- 32 ounces spaghetti sauce

- ½ teaspoon sea salt

- 8 ounces cottage cheese

- 16-ounce box lasagna noodles

- 3 cups shredded cheese (our favorite is Colby jack but you can also use mozzarella)

- ⅓ cup water

Instructions

1. In a large pot, cook hamburger meat with onion. Drain grease if necessary.

2. Stir in pasta sauce and salt.

3. Remove from heat and stir in cottage cheese.

4. Lay ⅓ of the lasagna noodles (uncooked) to cover the bottom of a 9x13 inch baking dish.

5. Pour ⅓ of the sauce mixture over the noodles and spread to cover the noodles.

6. Sprinkle ⅓ of the shredded cheese over the top.

7. Repeat these layers twice more.

8. Drizzle ⅓ cup water over the lasagna.

9. Cover tightly with foil.

10. Bake for one hour at 350°.

SIMPLE HASHBROWN AND EGG NESTS

Serves: 12 | Oven: 400°

Ingredients

- 15 ounces frozen shredded hashbrowns

- 8 eggs

- 2 Tablespoons dried minced onion

- 1 cup shredded cheese (we like Colby jack or pepper jack best, but any variety will work!)

- Sea salt and pepper to taste

Instructions

1. Mix ingredients together in a bowl until well combined.

2. Scoop mixture into prepared muffin tins (I find that it works best to melt a bit of oil in each tin so that the baked nests pop right out!)

3. Bake in a 400° oven for 30 minutes or until golden brown.

SIMPLE TUNA PATTIES

Serves: 6-8

Ingredients

- 15 ounces canned tuna in water, drained

- 2 eggs

- ¼ cup grated parmesan cheese

- 2 Tablespoons dried minced onions

- Sea salt and pepper to taste

- Oil for frying (I recommend palm shortening or refined coconut oil as these are both flavorless and remain stable at high temperatures.)

Instructions

1. In a bowl, stir together all ingredients except for the oil.

2. Heat about 3 Tablespoons of oil in a skillet.

3. Drop a large scoop full of tuna mixture into hot oil, pressing to flatten into a patty.

4. Cook for about 2 minutes on each side or until both sides of the tuna patty are golden brown.

5. Serve right away.

LAST MINUTE CREAMY BACON SPAGHETTI

Serves: 4-6

Ingredients

- 16 ounces whole grain spaghetti

- 1 pound uncooked bacon, cut into 1-inch pieces

- 4 ounces softened cream cheese, cut into cubes

- ½ cup Italian dressing*

- 4 Tablespoons grated parmesan cheese

Instructions

1. Cook spaghetti according to package directions.

2. In the meantime, cook bacon in a skillet.

3. Drain grease from bacon.

4. Drain water from spaghetti.

5. Immediately pour hot spaghetti into the skillet with cooked bacon.

6. Add remaining ingredients, stirring until cream cheese is melted and dish is well combined.

7. Serve right away.

*Italian Dressing Mix

Ingredients

- 1½ teaspoons garlic powder

- 1 Tablespoon onion powder

- 2 teaspoons oregano

- 1 Tablespoon dried parsley

- 2 teaspoons sea salt

- 1 teaspoon pepper

- ¼ teaspoon thyme

- ½ teaspoon dried celery flakes

Instructions

Shake ingredients together and store in a jar.

To make Italian salad dressing: Mix 2 Tablespoons dry mix with ¼ cup vinegar (I prefer red wine vinegar), 2 teaspoons water and ½ cup olive oil.

SIMPLE BUILD-A-SPANISH-RICE-BOWL

Serves: 6-8

Ingredients

- 1 pound cooked ground beef, seasoned with chili powder, garlic powder, and salt

- 2 cups cooked brown rice

- 1 can black beans

- 1 can sliced olives

- Shredded cheese

- Sour cream

- Salsa

- Fresh greens

- Cooked corn

Instructions

1. Set out any or all of the ingredients listed above, along with anything else your family might like.

2. Allow each person to fill their bowl the way they like.

SIMPLE OVEN ROASTED ROTISSERIE CHICKEN

Serves: 4-6 | Oven: 300°

Ingredients

- 3-4 pound whole chicken

- 3 Tablespoons softened butter

- 1 teaspoon sea salt

- 1 teaspoon ground pepper

- 1 teaspoon garlic powder

- 1 teaspoon onion powder

- 1 teaspoon thyme

- 1 teaspoon paprika

Instructions

1. Place chicken in a 9x13 inch baking dish.

2. Remove gizzards from the cavity. Discard them or save them to make broth later.

3. Spread or brush butter over the chicken.

4. Mix herbs and spices in a bowl, then rub them all over the chicken.

5. Bake uncovered, in a 300° oven for 2½ hours.

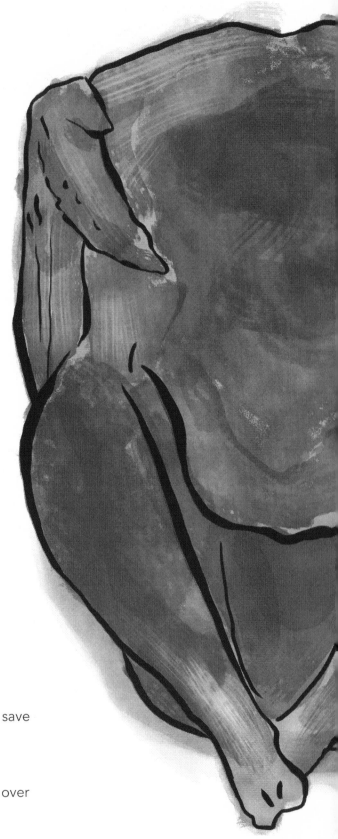

SIMPLE GREEN CHILE CHICKEN

Serves: 4-6 | Oven: 350°

Ingredients

- 2-3 pounds boneless chicken thighs or breasts
- 8 ounces softened cream cheese
- 1 cup shredded cheese (any variety)
- 4 ounces green chilies (no need to drain)
- ½ teaspoon garlic powder
- ½ teaspoon ground cumin
- ¼ teaspoon sea salt
- ¼ teaspoon ground black pepper

Instructions

1. Place chicken in a 9x13 inch dish.

2. Mix remaining ingredients (I do this quickly in my Blendtec), and spread the mixture over the chicken evenly.

3. Bake uncovered, in a 350° oven for 30 minutes.

SIMPLE TEX-MEX CREAMY CHICKEN

Serves: 6-8

Ingredients

- 2 pounds boneless chicken thighs or breasts

- 2 Tablespoons olive oil

- 1 Tablespoon chili powder

- Sea salt to taste

- 16 ounces salsa

- 15 ounces black beans

- 2 cups corn

- 2 cups sour cream

Instructions

1. In a skillet, brown chicken pieces in olive oil, seasoning them with chili powder and salt.

2. Once chicken is cooked through and through (about five minutes on each side) add salsa, black beans, and corn.

3. Simmer for about two minutes.

4. Remove from heat and stir in sour cream.

5. Serve over brown rice, pasta, or tortilla chips

FROM BURRITO BAR TO CASSEROLE

Serves: 6-8 | Oven: 275°-350°

Ingredients

- Leftover cooked chicken or hamburger (1-2 pounds)

- Leftover cooked rice (2-3 cups)

- Leftover beans (up to 2 cups)

- Salsa (2-3 cups)

- Sour Cream (2-3 cups)

- Shredded cheese (1-3 cups, optional)

Instructions

1. Stir these leftovers together, not worrying much about the measurements!

2. Spread the mixture into a 9x13 inch casserole dish.

3. Top it with cheese (optional).

4. Cover and refrigerate until ready to warm and serve. Or cover and freeze for up to two months.

5. When you are ready to serve this meal, cover it with foil and slide it into a cold oven.

6. Bake a refrigerated casserole at 350° for about 45 minutes. Bake a frozen casserole at 275° for 2-3 hours or until hot and bubbly.

SIMPLE GRILLED CHICKEN

Serves: 4-6

Ingredients

- 2-3 pounds boneless chicken thighs

- 2 cups of your favorite marinade (bbq, teriyaki, Italian dressing, etc.)

Instructions

1. Place chicken in a single layer in a 9x13 inch dish.

2. Spread dressing or sauce over the top.

3. Cover and allow chicken to marinate until grill time or for at least two hours (overnight is fine!)

4. Grill marinated chicken on low heat for 20-25 minutes, watching to be sure chicken is cooked evenly on both sides.

Homemade Teriyaki Sauce

Ingredients

- ¼ cup tamari soy sauce

- 1 cup water

- 1-2 teaspoons freshly grated ginger or dry ground ginger (more or less to taste)

- 2 Tablespoons honey

- 1 minced garlic clove

- 2 Tablespoons organic cornstarch

- ¼ cup cold water

Instructions

- Combine 1 cup water, soy sauce, honey, garlic and ginger in a saucepan and bring to a boil, stirring constantly.

- Dissolve cornstarch in ¼ cup cold water and add to sauce.

- Stir constantly and allow the sauce to thicken.

- If the sauce is too thick, add a little bit of water or soy sauce to thin.

*Italian Dressing Mix

Ingredients

- 1½ teaspoons garlic powder

- 1 Tablespoon onion powder

- 2 teaspoons oregano

- 1 Tablespoon dried parsley

- 2 teaspoons sea salt

- 1 teaspoon pepper

- ¼ teaspoon thyme

- ½ teaspoon dried celery flakes

Instructions

Shake ingredients together and store in a jar.

To make Italian salad dressing: Mix 2 Tablespoons dry mix with ¼ cup vinegar (I prefer red wine vinegar), 2 teaspoons water and ½ cup olive oil.

*Homemade Barbeque Sauce

Ingredients

- ¾ cup ketchup (I use an organic, no high fructose corn syrup variety)

- 2 Tablespoons minced onion

- ¼ teaspoon garlic powder

- 1 teaspoon liquid smoke

- 1 Tablespoon molasses, honey or sucanat (optional)

Instructions

- Mix ingredients in a small sauce pan.

- Simmer for a few minutes until flavors are blended.

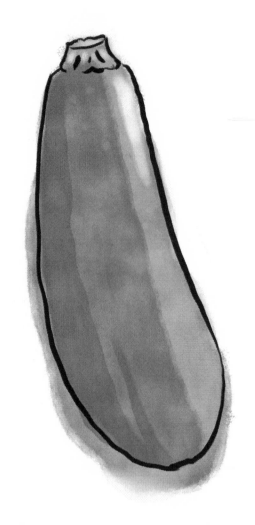

SIMPLE VEGGIE FRITTERS

Makes 12 patties

Ingredients

- 2 small zucchini

- 2 medium-sized carrots

- 2 Tablespoons dried minced onion

- 1 cup grated cheese (we like Colby jack or cheddar best for these but any variety will work)

- 1 cup flour (we use freshly ground hard white wheat for these but you can use your favorite!)

- 1 cup milk

- 1 egg

- ½ teaspoon cayenne pepper (optional)

- Sea salt and pepper to taste

- Oil for frying (I recommend palm shortening or refined coconut oil as they are flavorless and remain stable at high temperatures.)

Instructions

1. Grate the zucchini and carrots into a bowl.

2. Add remaining ingredients and mix well.

3. Heat about 3 Tablespoons of oil in a skillet.

4. Scoop veggie mixture into hot oil, pressing down to make patties.

5. Fry until each side is golden brown, about 2 minutes each.

SIMPLE LEMON GARLIC CHICKEN LEGS

Serves: 6-8 | Oven: 425°

Ingredients

- 10-12 chicken legs
- 1 large-sized lemon
- 2 teaspoons garlic powder
- 1 teaspoon sea salt
- ½ teaspoon paprika
- ½ teaspoon black pepper

Instructions

1. Lay chicken legs in a 9x13 inch baking dish.
2. In a medium-sized bowl, juice and zest the lemon.
3. Add remaining ingredients to the lemon juice/zest and stir.
4. Pour the mixture over the chicken.
5. Bake uncovered, in a 425° oven for 35-45 minutes or until juices run clear.

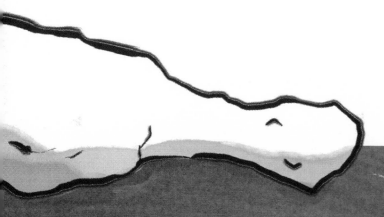

SIMPLE THREE-CHEESE SPAGHETTI

Serves: 6-8

Ingredients

- 16 ounces whole grain spaghetti noodles

- 1 tablespoon olive oil

- 1½ tablespoons minced garlic

- 1 cup freshly shredded pepper jack cheese (or cheddar if you want to avoid the spice)

- ½ cup freshly shredded parmesan cheese

- 4 Tablespoons cream cheese

- 1 cup heavy cream

- Salt and pepper to taste

Instructions

1. Cook spaghetti noodles according to package; drain.

2. While noodles are cooking, saute garlic and olive oil for 1-2 minutes in a medium sauce pan.

3. Remove from heat and add remaining ingredients to the pan.

4. Place back on the burner, and cook and stir sauce ingredients until cheeses are melted and sauce is smooth and creamy.

5. Pour cheese sauce over the cooked spaghetti noodles and serve.

SIMPLE CHEESEBURGER HASHBROWN CUPS OR CASSEROLE

Serves: 24 cups or 6-8 servings | Oven: 350° or 400°

Ingredients

- 1 pound ground beef, lamb, or turkey

- 15 ounces frozen shredded hashbrowns

- ½ - 1 cup ketchup (depending on how much your family likes ketchup)

- 3 eggs

- 3 Tablespoons dried minced onion

- 2 cups shredded cheese (we like Colby jack or pepper jack best, but any variety will work!)

- Sea salt and pepper to taste

Instructions

1. Brown meat in a skillet until no longer pink.

2. Mix cooked meat and remaining ingredients together in a bowl until well combined.

- **For Cups:** Scoop mixture into prepared muffin tins (I find that it works best to melt a bit of oil in each tin so that the baked nests pop right out!) Bake in a 400° oven for 30 minutes or until golden brown.

- **For Casserole:** Spread mixture into a 9x13 inch baking dish. Bake uncovered in a 350° oven for 45 minutes or until golden brown.

SIMPLE CREAMY LAYERED ENCHILADAS (FOR OVEN OR CROCK POT)

Serves: 4-6 | Oven: 350°

Ingredients

- 1 pound ground beef

- Sea salt to taste

- 2 cups salsa

- 1½ cups sour cream

- 2 cups shredded cheddar cheese, divided

- 8 whole wheat or corn tortillas

Instructions

1. Brown meat. Stir in salt, salsa, sour cream, and ½ cup of cheese.

2. Lay 4 tortillas in the bottom of a 9x13 inch baking dish.

3. Spread half of meat mixture over tortillas.

- Layer again with the 4 remaining tortillas.

- Spread remaining meat mixture over tortillas.

- Top with 1½ cups cheese.

- Bake uncovered at 350° for 20-25 minutes.

- OR Layer ingredients into a crock pot. Cook on Low for 6-7 hours or on Hi for 4 hours.

SIMPLE HAM AND HASHBROWN CASSEROLE

Serves: 6-8 | Oven: 350°

Ingredients

- 3 cups ham cut into bite-sized pieces

- 3 cups sour cream

- 3 Tablespoons dried minced onion

- Sea salt and pepper to taste

- 1 (28 ounce) bag of frozen shredded hashbrowns

- 2 cups shredded cheddar or Colby jack cheese

Instructions

1. In a large bowl, stir together ham, shredded cheese, sour cream, onion, and salt and pepper.

2. Fold in frozen hashbrowns until all ingredients are well combined.

3. Spread mixture into a 9x13 inch baking dish or into a large crock pot.

4. Sprinkle with shredded cheese.

- **Oven Baking:** Bake uncovered in a 350° oven for 45-60 minutes or until casserole is lightly browned and bubbly.

- **Crock Pot Method:** Cook on low for 6 hours or on hi for 3 hours.

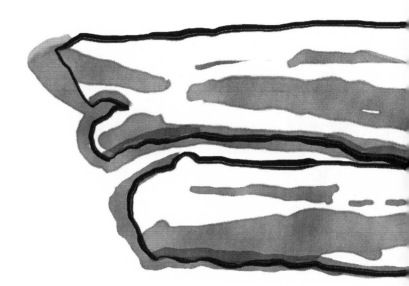

SIMPLE BROCCOLI BACON CHICKEN

Serves: 6-8 | Oven: 400°

Ingredients

- 2 pounds boneless, skinless chicken thighs or breasts

- 1 head fresh broccoli

- ½ pound cooked bacon crumbles

- 2 cups shredded cheese (any of your favorites will work!)

Instructions

1. Lay chicken in the bottom of a 9x13 inch casserole dish.

2. Cut broccoli into florets and place them on top of the chicken.

3. Sprinkle bacon crumbles over the chicken and broccoli.

4. Sprinkle cheese over the top of the casserole.

5. Bake in a 400° oven for 30 minutes or until chicken has cooked through and juice runs clear.

SIMPLE MAKE-AHEAD PARMESAN MEATBALLS

Serves: 16-20 meatballs | Oven: 350°

Ingredients

- 2 pounds ground beef or turkey

- 2 eggs

- 3 Tablespoons dried minced onion

- ½ cup shredded (or grated) parmesan cheese

- 1 teaspoon sea salt

- ¼ teaspoon ground pepper

- ½ teaspoon garlic powder

Instructions

1. Mix all ingredients together until well combined.

2. Scoop any size balls out onto a cookie sheet (I use a large scoop).

3. Bake in a 350° oven for 30-45 minutes or until the meat is no longer pink.

4. Serve right away, or refrigerate or freeze baked meatballs to easily reheat for a meal later.

5. OR, freeze the prepared meatballs UNBAKED, thaw as needed, and bake as directed.

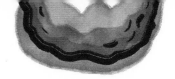

SIMPLE SAUCY PARMESAN MEATBALLS

Serves: 4-6 | Oven: 350°

Ingredients

- 1-2 pounds of pre-made Parmesan Meatballs (opposite page)

- 16 ounces of your favorite sauce

- 12 ounces cooked pasta

Instructions

1. Reheat or bake meatballs as directed.

2. Pour sauce over meatballs and simmer until heated through.

3. Serve over your favorite prepared pasta. OR

4. Serve with rice or potatoes if you like!

SIMPLE POPCORN CHICKEN

Serves: 4-6 | Oven: 350°

Ingredients

- 3-6 large boneless, skinless chicken thighs or breasts

- ¾ cup whole grain flour (I use freshly ground white wheat, but you can use any flour you like!)

- ½ teaspoon sea salt

- ½ teaspoon garlic powder

- butter

Instructions

1. In a medium-sized bowl stir together flour, salt, and garlic powder.

2. Using kitchen shears, cut chicken into tiny bite-sized pieces.

3. Toss chicken in flour mixture to coat well.

4. Smear a thick layer of butter on the bottom of a 9x13 inch baking dish.

5. Pour coated chicken into the dish, spreading so that they are in a single layer.

6. Bake at 350° for 10 minutes. Stir chicken and bake another 10 minutes.

Need some dipping sauce to go with your Simple Popcorn Chicken? Here are our favorites:

Homemade Barbeque Sauce

Ingredients

- ¾ cup ketchup (I use an organic, no high fructose corn syrup variety)

- 2 Tablespoons minced onion

- ¼ teaspoon garlic powder

- 1 teaspoon liquid smoke

- 1 Tablespoon molasses, honey or sucanat (optional)

Instructions

- Mix ingredients in a small sauce pan.

- Simmer for a few minutes until flavors are blended.

Ranch Dip/Dressing

Ingredients

- 5 Tablespoons dried minced onions

- 7 teaspoons parsley flakes

- 4 teaspoons sea salt

- 1 teaspoon garlic powder

Instructions

- Mix together and store in an air tight container.

- For dressing: Mix 2 Tablespoons dry mix with 1 cup mayonnaise and 1 cup buttermilk or sour cream.

- For dip: Mix 2 Tablespoons dry mix with 2 cups sour cream or Creme Fraiche.

- Mix up a few hours before serving, so the flavors all blend nicely.

Spicy Ranch Dressing

Ingredients

- 1 cup homemade ranch dressing (because it is good for you and delicious)

- 1-3 Tablespoons of your favorite hot sauce like Tabasco, Cholula, or Sriracha

- 1 teaspoon chili powder

- 1 teaspoon cumin

Instructions

- Mix together, and enjoy.

Want toasted tortillas? Simply warm them in a skillet over low heat for about 1 minute on each side until they turn lightly brown and barely crispy!

SIMPLE POPCORN CHICKEN TACOS

Serves: 4-6 | Oven: 350°

Ingredients

- 1 pound pre-made popcorn chicken (See previous page)

- 8 whole grain flour or corn tortillas

- Fresh taco fixins like tomatoes, lettuce, black beans, sweet peppers, corn, cilantro, onions, salsa, olives, etc

- Shredded cheese

Instructions

1. Rewarm popcorn chicken.

2. Prepare taco fixins and set out a buffet for each person to build Simple Popcorn Chicken Tacos per their preference!

SIMPLE (MOSTLY REAL FOOD) TATER TOT CASSEROLE

Serves: 6-8 | Oven: 425°

Ingredients

- 1½ - 2 pounds hamburger meat

- 1 medium onion or 3 Tablespoons dried minced onion

- 1 teaspoon garlic powder

- Sea salt to taste (we find it takes quite a lot of this good salt to provide good flavor in this meal!)

- 4 cups cooked green beans

- 3 cups sour cream

- 3 cups shredded cheese (we use Colby jack)

- 3 cups tater tots

Instructions

1. Brown hamburger meat with onion, garlic, and salt.

2. Mix cooked meat with green beans and sour cream and spread mixture into a 9x13 inch casserole dish.

3. Spread shredded cheese over the mixture.

4. Top with frozen tater tots.

5. Bake in a 425° oven for 30-40 minutes or until bubbly.

SIMPLE MAKE-AHEAD PARMESAN BURGERS

Serves: 8

Ingredients

- 2 pounds ground beef or turkey

- 2 eggs

- 3 Tablespoons dried minced onion

- ½ cup shredded (or grated) parmesan cheese

- 1 teaspoon sea salt

- ¼ teaspoon ground pepper

- ½ teaspoon garlic powder

Instructions

1. Mix all ingredients together until well combined.

2. Press together burger-sized patties.

3. Fry in a skillet or on a grill for 8-12 minutes or until the meat is no longer pink.

4. Serve right away, or refrigerate or freeze cooked burgers to easily reheat for a meal later.

5. OR, freeze the prepared raw burgers, thaw as needed, and fry as directed.

SIMPLE HEARTY BEAN CASSEROLE

Serves: 4-6

Ingredients

- 1 pound hamburger meat
- ½ pound bacon, cut into pieces.
- 2 Tablespoons dry minced onion
- 3 Tablespoons ketchup
- 2 15-ounce cans of Baked Beans

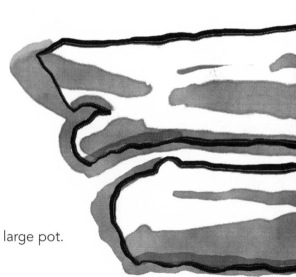

Instructions

1. Cook hamburger meat, bacon, and onion together in a large pot.
2. Drain excess grease if necessary.
3. Stir beans and ketchup into cooked meat.
4. Heat until bubbly.
5. Serve and eat!

SIMPLE CROCK POT
RECIPES

SIMPLE SHREDDED RANCH CHICKEN

Serves: 4-6

Ingredients

- 2-3 pounds boneless chicken thighs or breasts

- 2 Tablespoons olive oil

- 3 Tablespoons Taco Seasoning (opposite page)

- 3 Tablespoons dry Ranch Seasoning (opposite page)

Instructions

1. Place chicken in the bottom of a crock pot.

2. Drizzle on olive oil.

3. Sprinkle on seasoning mixes.

4. Cook on low for 6-8 hours.

5. Shred chicken and serve with favorite taco toppings on hard or soft shells.

Homemade Taco Seasoning

Ingredients

- ½ cup chili powder
- ¼ cup onion powder
- ⅛ cup ground cumin
- 1 Tablespoon garlic powder
- 1 Tablespoon paprika
- 1 Tablespoon sea salt

Put all ingredients into a jar and shake!

Ranch Seasoning

Ingredients

- 5 Tablespoons dried minced onions
- 7 teaspoons parsley flakes
- 4 teaspoons sea salt
- 1 teaspoon garlic powder

Instructions

- Mix together and store in an air tight container.
- For dressing: Mix 2 Tablespoons dry mix with 1 cup mayonnaise and 1 cup buttermilk or sour cream.
- For dip: Mix 2 Tablespoons dry mix with 2 cups sour cream or Creme Fraiche.
- Mix up a few hours before serving, so the flavors all blend nicely.

SIMPLE CREAMY CHICKEN STEW IN THE CROCK POT

Serves: 4-6

Ingredients

- 1 pound boneless chicken breasts or thighs

- 4-5 small potatoes (I prefer red or gold)

- 1 pound carrots

- 1 cup heavy whipping cream

- ½ cup sour cream

- 1 cup chicken broth

- 3 Tablespoons dry ranch dressing mix*

- Sea salt and pepper to taste

Instructions

1. Cut chicken, potatoes, and carrots into bite-sized pieces and stir together in a crock pot.

2. Salt and pepper to taste.

3. In a bowl combine cream, sour cream, chicken broth, and ranch dressing mix.

4. Pour mixture over the chicken and veggies.

5. Cook on high for 3-4 hours or low for 5-7 hours.

*Ranch Seasoning

Ingredients

- 5 Tablespoons dried minced onions

- 7 teaspoons parsley flakes

- 4 teaspoons sea salt

- 1 teaspoon garlic powder

Instructions

- Mix together and store in an air tight container.

- For dressing: Mix 2 Tablespoons dry mix with 1 cup mayonnaise and 1 cup buttermilk or sour cream.

- For dip: Mix 2 Tablespoons dry mix with 2 cups sour cream or Creme Fraiche.

- Mix up a few hours before serving, so the flavors all blend nicely.

SIMPLE CROCK POT PIZZA CASSEROLE

Serves: 4-6

Ingredients

- 16 ounces whole grain pasta (uncooked)

- 50 ounces pizza or spaghetti sauce

- 2 cups shredded cheese

- 6 ounces pepperoni

- Optional: additional cooked meat, sliced olives, chopped sweet pepper, and/or sliced mushrooms

Instructions

1. Stir uncooked pasta and pizza sauce in a crock pot.

2. Cook on low for 3-4 hours.

3. Stir.

4. Top with shredded cheese and pepperoni.

5. Cook for an additional 10 minutes on low to melt cheese.

SIMPLE HAWAIIAN CROCK POT CHICKEN

Serves: 4-6

Ingredients

- 2-3 pounds boneless chicken thighs or breasts

- 8 ounces crushed or chunk pineapple, drained

- 2 cups barbecue sauce*

Instructions

1. Place chicken (frozen or thawed) in the bottom of a crock pot.

2. Top with pineapple and barbecue sauce.

3. Cook on high for 3-4 hours or low for 6-8 hours.

4. Shred chicken before serving.

5. Serve over rice if you like.

*Homemade Barbeque Sauce

Ingredients

- ¾ cup ketchup (I use an organic, no high fructose corn syrup variety)

- 2 Tablespoons minced onion

- ¼ teaspoon garlic powder

- 1 teaspoon liquid smoke

- 1 Tablespoon molasses, honey or sucanat (optional)

Instructions

- Mix ingredients in a small sauce pan.

- Simmer for a few minutes until flavors are blended.

SIMPLE CROCK POT BBQ SPARERIBS

Serves: 4-6

Ingredients

- 3-4 pound package of beef or pork spareribs

- 1-2 cups of your favorite BBQ Sauce (opposite page)

Instructions

1. Place spareribs in your crockpot. I typically have to fold them over to get them to fit.

2. Spread BBQ Sauce over the meat.

3. Cook on low for 7-8 hours or until meat is falling off the bone.

SIMPLE OVERNIGHT SAUCY CHICKEN

Serves: 4-6

Ingredients

- 1-3 pounds frozen, boneless chicken thighs or breasts

- 1-2 cups of your favorite sauce (bbq, teriyaki, sweet and sour, etc) (see opposite page)

Instructions

1. Place frozen chicken in a crock pot.

2. Pour sauce over the chicken.

3. Cook on low for 7-10 hours overnight.

Homemade Barbeque Sauce

Ingredients

- ¾ cup ketchup (I use an organic, no high fructose corn syrup variety)

- 2 Tablespoons minced onion

- ¼ teaspoon garlic powder

- 1 teaspoon liquid smoke

- 1 Tablespoon molasses, honey or sucanat (optional)

Instructions

- Mix ingredients in a small sauce pan.

- Simmer for a few minutes until flavors are blended.

Homemade Teriyaki Sauce

Ingredients

- ¼ cup tamari soy sauce

- 1 cup water

- 1-2 teaspoons freshly grated ginger or dry ground ginger (more or less to taste)

- 2 Tablespoons honey

- 1 minced garlic clove

- 2 Tablespoons organic cornstarch

- ¼ cup cold water

Instructions

- Combine 1 cup water, soy sauce, honey, garlic and ginger in a saucepan and bring to a boil, stirring constantly.

- Dissolve cornstarch in ¼ cup cold water and add to sauce.

- Stir constantly and allow the sauce to thicken.

- If the sauce is too thick, add a little bit of water or soy sauce to thin.

SIMPLE 3-CHEESE CROCK POT PASTA

Serves: 4-6

Ingredients

- 2 jars of your favorite spaghetti sauce (25-32 ounces each)

- 15 ounces ricotta cheese

- 2 cups grated parmesan cheese

- 1 cup grated mozzarella, cheddar, or Colby jack cheese

- 1 pound whole grain pasta (uncooked), any shape

- Sea salt to taste

Instructions

1. Dump all ingredients into a crock pot and stir well.

2. Cook on low for 4-6 hours or on high for 2-3 hours or until pasta is tender.

SIMPLE CROCK POT TACO PASTA

Serves: 6-8

Ingredients

- 1 pound ground taco meat (cooked)
- 16 ounces whole grain pasta (uncooked)
- 32 ounces salsa
- 2 cups water
- ½ teaspoon sea salt
- 2 cups shredded cheese

Instructions

1. Stir all ingredients into a crock pot.
2. Cook on low for 4 hours.
3. Stir mixture.
4. Top with cheese and let sit for 5-10 minutes or until cheese is melted.

THE EASIEST MASHED POTATOES IN THE WORLD

Serves: 6-8

Ingredients

- 5 pounds potatoes (I prefer yukon gold)

- 1 cup whole milk, half-and-half, or cream

- 2 cups sour cream

- ¼-½ cup butter

- Sea salt to taste

Instructions

1. Scrub, but don't peel the potatoes

2. Cook them in a crock pot on low for 8-10 hours or on high for 5 hours.

3. Mash soft potatoes directly in the crock with a potato masher.

4. While mashing, dump in the milk, sour cream, butter, and salt.

5. Continue mashing until potatoes have reached desired consistency.

SIMPLE CROCK POT CREAMY STEW MEAT

Serves: 6-8

Ingredients

- 2-3 pounds beef stew meat
- 3 Tablespoons Ranch Dressing Mix*
- 2 Tablespoons Onion Soup Mix**
- ½ cup water
- ½ cup butter
- 2 cups heavy whipping cream

Instructions

1. In a crock pot, stir together stew meat, seasoning mixes, and water.
2. Put a stick of butter on top.
3. Place lid on crock pot and cook on low for 6-7 hours.
4. Add cream and heat for another 10 minutes.
5. Serve over rice or pasta

**Homemade Onion Soup Mix

Ingredients

- ⅔ cup dried, minced onion
- 3 teaspoons parsley flakes
- 2 teaspoons onion powder
- 2 teaspoons turmeric (optional)
- 1 teaspoon celery salt
- 1 teaspoon sea salt
- 1 teaspoon sucanat (or sugar if you prefer)
- ½ teaspoon ground pepper

Instructions

- Mix all ingredients in a jar, then give the jar a good shake.
- I'd recommend shaking the jar to mix the ingredients well before each use.
- Use 4 Tablespoons Onion Soup Mix in a recipe in place of 1 packet of onion soup mix. (I actually found that 2 Tablespoons was plenty in a beef stew recipe I tried.)
- Store this in a dry, cool place.

*Ranch Seasoning

Ingredients

- 5 Tablespoons dried minced onions
- 7 teaspoons parsley flakes
- 4 teaspoons sea salt
- 1 teaspoon garlic powder

Instructions

- Mix together and store in an air tight container.
- For dressing: Mix 2 Tablespoons dry mix with 1 cup mayonnaise and 1 cup buttermilk or sour cream.
- For dip: Mix 2 Tablespoons dry mix with 2 cups sour cream or Creme Fraiche.
- Mix up a few hours before serving, so the flavors all blend nicely.

SIMPLE BARBECUE BEEF ROAST

Serves: 6-8

Ingredients

- 3-4 pound beef roast, frozen or thawed
- 1-2 cups BBQ sauce*
- 1-2 medium onions

Instructions

1. Place roast in a crock pot.
2. Douse the meat with barbecue sauce.
3. Quarter the onion and place in the crock pot.
4. Cover and cook on low for 10 hours if frozen or 8 hours if thawed.

*Homemade Barbeque Sauce

Ingredients

- ¾ cup ketchup (I use an organic, no high fructose corn syrup variety)
- 2 Tablespoons minced onion
- ¼ teaspoon garlic powder
- 1 teaspoon liquid smoke
- 1 Tablespoon molasses, honey or sucanat (optional)

Instructions

- Mix ingredients in a small sauce pan.
- Simmer for a few minutes until flavors are blended.

THE SIMPLEST WHITE CHICKEN CHILI

Serves: 6-8

Ingredients

- 1-2 pounds boneless Chicken thighs or breasts

- 2 15-ounce cans Black Beans (drained)

- 2 10-ounce cans Rotel (Diced Tomatoes and Green Chiles)

- 2 cups Frozen Corn

- 3 Tablespoons Ranch Dressing Mix*

- 1 Tablespoon Chili Powder

- 2 8-ounce packages Cream Cheese

Instructions

1. Place chicken (frozen or thawed) in the bottom of a crock pot.

2. Add beans, Rotel, corn, and seasonings over the chicken and stir.

3. Place cream cheese on top of the mixture.

4. Cook on low for 7-8 hours or on high for 3-4 hours.

5. Remove chicken and shred, then stir it back into the soup.

*Ranch Seasoning

Ingredients

- 5 Tablespoons dried minced onions

- 7 teaspoons parsley flakes

- 4 teaspoons sea salt

- 1 teaspoon garlic powder

Instructions

- Mix together and store in an air tight container.

- For dressing: Mix 2 Tablespoons dry mix with 1 cup mayonnaise and 1 cup buttermilk or sour cream.

- For dip: Mix 2 Tablespoons dry mix with 2 cups sour cream or Creme Fraiche.

- Mix up a few hours before serving, so the flavors all blend nicely.

SIMPLE CROCK POT APPLESAUCE BBQ CHICKEN

Serves: 4-6

Ingredients

- 2 pounds boneless chicken thighs or breasts
- ⅔ cup natural applesauce
- ⅔ cup BBQ sauce*
- Sea salt to taste
- Chili powder to taste

Instructions

1. Place chicken pieces at the bottom of a crock pot.
2. Sprinkle salt and chili powder over chicken.
3. Drizzle on applesauce and bbq sauce.
4. Cover and cook on low for 5 hours.
5. Serve over rice or potatoes.

*Homemade Barbeque Sauce

Ingredients

- ¾ cup ketchup (I use an organic, no high fructose corn syrup variety)
- 2 Tablespoons minced onion
- ¼ teaspoon garlic powder
- 1 teaspoon liquid smoke
- 1 Tablespoon molasses, honey or sucanat (optional)

Instructions

- Mix ingredients in a small sauce pan.
- Simmer for a few minutes until flavors are blended.

SIMPLE OVERNIGHT MELT-IN-YOUR-MOUTH BEEF ROAST

Serves: 4-6

Ingredients

- 3-4 pound beef roast
- 3 Tablespoons Worcestershire sauce
- 3 Tablespoons Onion Soup Mix (recipe below)
- ½ cup water

Instructions

1. Put roast in the bottom of a crock pot. (Roast can be frozen or thawed.)
2. Pour Worcestershire sauce, Onion Soup Mix, and water over the roast.
3. Cook on low for 10-12 hours.

*Homemade Onion Soup Mix

Ingredients

- ⅔ cup dried, minced onion
- 3 teaspoons parsley flakes
- 2 teaspoons onion powder
- 2 teaspoons turmeric (optional)
- 1 teaspoon celery salt
- 1 teaspoon sea salt
- 1 teaspoon sucanat (or sugar if you prefer)
- ½ teaspoon ground pepper

Instructions

- Mix all ingredients in a jar, then give the jar a good shake.
- I'd recommend shaking the jar to mix the ingredients well before each use.
- Use 4 Tablespoons Onion Soup Mix in a recipe in place of 1 packet of onion soup mix. (I actually found that 2 Tablespoons was plenty in a beef stew recipe I tried.)
- Store this in a dry, cool place.

SIMPLE CROCK POT SALSA SHREDDED BEEF

Serves: 6-8

Ingredients

- 3-4 pound beef or lamb roast

- 16 ounces salsa

Instructions

1. Place frozen or thawed roast into a crock pot.

2. Pour salsa over the top.

3. Cook in a crock pot on low for 10-12 hours if frozen. If thawed, cook for 8-10 hours on low.

4. Shred meat and serve.

SIMPLE 5-MINUTE CHEESY POTATOES AND BEEF

Serves: 6-8

Ingredients

- 1-2 pounds ground beef

- 30 ounces frozen hashbrowns (or 5 medium potatoes sliced thinly)

- 2 Tablespoons dried minced onion

- 1 teaspoon paprika

- 1 teaspoon garlic powder

- 1 teaspoon sea salt

- 3 cups shredded cheese (we use Colby jack)

- ½ cup chicken or beef broth

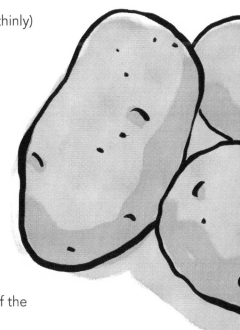

Instructions

1. Brown hamburger meat in a skillet on the stove-top.

2. In a large crock pot, layer ½ of the potatoes followed by ½ of the cooked meat.

3. Sprinkle with 1 Tablespoon minced onion, ½ teaspoon paprika, ½ teaspoon garlic powder, ½ teaspoon sea salt, and 1½ cups shredded cheese.

- Repeat with another layer of potatoes, meat, seasonings, and cheese.

- Drizzle broth over the ingredients and put the lid on the crock pot.

- Cook on hi for 4 hours.

SIMPLE CHEESEBURGER NOODLE CROCK POT DINNER

Serves: 4-6

Ingredients

- 1 pound hamburger meat

- 1 small chopped onion OR 3 Tablespoons dried minced onion

- 12 ounces whole grain egg noodles (uncooked)

- 2 cups sour cream

- 30 ounces tomato sauce

- 1 cup water

- Sea salt and pepper to taste

- ½ teaspoon garlic powder

- 1 teaspoon parsley flakes

- 2 cups shredded cheese (we like cheddar or Colby jack)

Instructions

1. In a skillet, cook hamburger and onion together until meat is no longer pink. Drain if necessary.

2. Stir cooked meat along with all other ingredients into a crock pot.

3. Cover and cook on low for 3-4 hours.

SIMPLE 5-MINUTE CHICKEN

Serves: 2-3 meals

Ingredients

- 3 pounds boneless chicken thighs or breasts

- Any seasonings you like (I use garlic powder, sea salt, paprika, and parsley flakes)

Instructions

1. Place chicken in a crock pot and sprinkle with any herbs or spices you like.

2. Cook on low for 4-5 hours.

3. Shred chicken to use in any of your favorite recipes or to serve in tacos, or even as a main dish as-is!

Looking for more recipes?

These Instant Pot recipes work in the Crock Pot, too!

SIMPLE INSTANT POT RECIPES

SIMPLE CREAMY PASTA IN THE INSTANT POT

Serves: 6-8

Ingredients

- 1 pound ground beef, turkey, or venison

- 2 Tablespoons minced onion

- 1 pound whole grain pasta, any shape

- 24 ounces spaghetti sauce

- 3 cups water

- Sea salt to taste

- 1 cup parmesan cheese

- 1½ cups heavy whipping cream

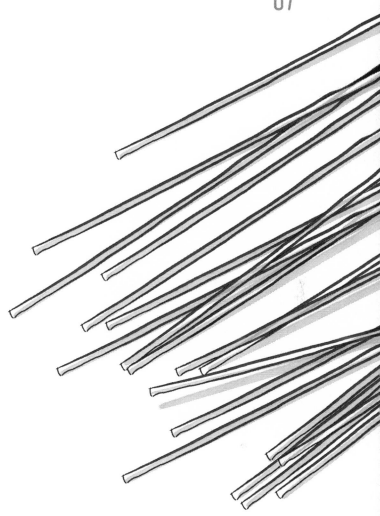

Instructions

1. Cook ground meat and onion together until meat is no longer pink. (I usually have meat pre-cooked to stir into this recipe. But you can use the sauté function on your instant pot to make this a one-dish meal.)

2. Stir cooked meat and dry pasta into the instant pot.

3. Salt liberally.

4. Pour on spaghetti sauce and water, stirring until barely combined.

5. Seal instant pot and cook on "hi" pressure, manual for 5 minutes.

6. Do a quick release of pressure to open the lid.

7. Stir in parmesan cheese and cream.

8. Serve!

SIMPLE HASHBROWN CASSEROLE

Serves: 6-8

Ingredients

- 1 pound cooked meat (hamburger, ham, bacon, sausage, or any of your choosing!)

- 2 cups shredded cheddar or Colby jack cheese

- 3 cups sour cream

- 3 Tablespoons Ranch Dressing Mix*

- 1 bag of frozen shredded hashbrowns

Instructions

1. In a large bowl, stir together cooked meat, shredded cheese, sour cream, and ranch dressing mix.

2. Fold in frozen hashbrowns until all ingredients are well combined.

- **Instant Pot Method:** Add ½ cup water to the bottom of the Instant Pot before adding remaining ingredients. Cook for 15 minutes on manual mode, hi pressure.

- **Oven Baking:** Bake uncovered in a 350° oven for 45-60 minutes or until casserole is lightly browned and bubbly.

- **Crock Pot Method:** Cook on low for 6 hours or on hi for 3 hours.

*Ranch Seasoning

Ingredients

- 5 Tablespoons dried minced onions

- 7 teaspoons parsley flakes

- 4 teaspoons sea salt

- 1 teaspoon garlic powder

Instructions

- Mix together and store in an air tight container.

- For dressing: Mix 2 Tablespoons dry mix with 1 cup mayonnaise and 1 cup buttermilk or sour cream.

- For dip: Mix 2 Tablespoons dry mix with 2 cups sour cream or Creme Fraiche.

- Mix up a few hours before serving, so the flavors all blend nicely.

SIMPLE LASAGNA CASSEROLE

Serves: 6-8

Ingredients

- 16 ounces whole grain pasta (uncooked), any shape

- 1 pound cooked hamburger meat

- 50 ounces spaghetti sauce

- 1 cup water

- 16 ounces cottage cheese

- Sea salt to taste

- 2 cups shredded cheese (your favorite)

Instructions

1. Stir uncooked pasta, spaghetti sauce, water, cooked meat, sea salt, and cottage cheese in a crock pot or instant pot. Cook as follows:

- **Instant Pot Method:** Cook on Manual at high pressure for 5 minutes.

- **Crock Pot Method:** Cook on low for 3-4 hours.

2. Once time is up for either Crock Pot or Instant Pot, stir mixture and top with cheese, covering dish so the cheese will melt.

SIMPLE CHILI MAC

Serves: 4-6

Ingredients

- 16 ounces whole grain pasta (uncooked), any shape

- 1 pound cooked hamburger meat

- 50 ounces spaghetti sauce

- 1 cup water

- 16 ounces cottage cheese

- Sea salt to taste

- 2 cups shredded cheese (your favorite)

Instructions

1. Stir chili, uncooked pasta, water and salt into Instant Pot, Crock Pot, or large cooking pot.

- **Instant Pot Method:** Cook at high pressure for 6 minutes.

- **Stove Top:** Cook on low heat, covered, stirring every few minutes until pasta is tender.

- **Crock Pot Method:** Cook on low for 4 hours or hi for 2.5 hours.

2. Top casserole with cheese and allow it to melt before serving.

THE EASIEST WAY TO MAKE BEEF ROAST IN THE INSTANT POT

Serves: 6-8

Ingredients

- 3 pound beef roast

- 2 Tablespoons Worcestershire sauce

- 1 medium-sized onion

- Sea salt and pepper to taste

- 5-8 medium-sized carrots

- 1 cup water

Instructions

1. Place roast on the metal trivet in your Instant Pot.

2. Pour 1 cup water into the bottom of the pot.

3. Cut onion into fourths and place in the pot.

4. Peel carrots, cut them in half, then place them on the roast.

5. Salt liberally, pepper as you like.

6. Place the lid on the Instant Pot and seal it.

7. Cook it at High Pressure, Manual Setting, for 70 minutes.

8. Allow the pressure to release naturally, or do a quick release after 15 minutes.

9. Shred meat and serve!

Add 3ish pounds of scrubbed and cut potatoes to the pot if you like. :)

SIMPLE ONE-DISH CHICKEN FLORENTINE

Serves: 6-8

Ingredients

- 1½ pounds boneless chicken thighs or breasts

- 3 cloves fresh garlic, minced or 1 Tablespoon garlic powder

- Sea salt to taste

- 6 cups fresh spinach leaves

- 16 ounces whole grain spaghetti (uncooked)

- 2 cups heavy whipping cream

- 4 cups chicken broth

- 3 cups shredded mozzarella cheese

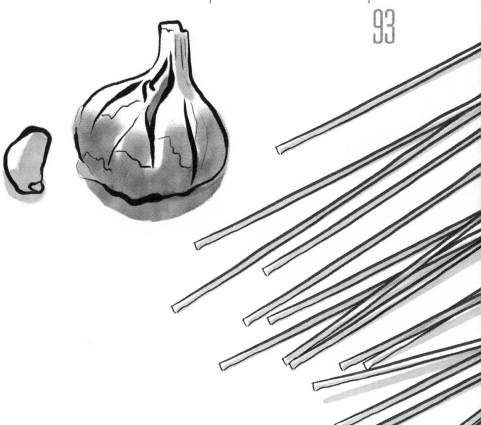

Instructions

1. Cut chicken into bite-sized pieces. (I use kitchen shears for this which makes it super fast!)

2. Place prepared chicken in the bottom of your Instant Pot or Crock Pot.

3. Sprinkle with garlic, salt, and spinach leaves.

4. Break spaghetti noodles in half and place on top.

5. Pour on chicken broth and cream.

6. Top with shredded cheese.

- **Instant Pot:** Seal Instant Pot and cook on the "Poultry" setting for 15 minutes, doing a quick release after the time runs out.

- **Crock Pot:** Cook in a Crock Pot on low for 6 hours.

7. Stir and serve.

8. Garnish with grated parmesan if you like!

SIMPLE 10-MINUTE INSTANT POT MAC AND CHEESE

Serves: 4-6

Ingredients

- 16 ounces whole grain pasta (any shape)

- 4 cups water

- 4 Tablespoons butter (always butter, never margarine, amen, hallelujah)

- 2 teaspoons sea salt

- 1 cup heavy whipping cream

- 3 cups shredded cheese (we love Colby jack)

Instructions

1. Stir uncooked pasta, water, butter, and salt in your instant pot.

2. Seal and cook on manual, high pressure for 4 minutes.

3. Quick release the pressure.

4. Open the pot and stir in the cream and cheese until melted and creamy.

SIMPLE CREAMY CHICKEN SOUP

Serves: 4-6

Ingredients

- 1-2 pounds boneless chicken thighs or breasts

- 10-ounce can Rotel

- 32 ounces (4 cups) chicken broth

- 1 teaspoon sea salt

- 1 teaspoon paprika

- 8 ounces softened cream cheese

- 1 cup heavy whipping cream

- 2 cups shredded Colby jack or cheddar cheese

Instructions

Place chicken, Rotel, broth, salt, and paprika into an Instant Pot or Crock Pot.

- **For Instant Pot:** Seal and cook on manual at high pressure for 15 minutes. Quick release.

- **For Crock Pot:** Cook ingredients on low for 6-8 hours or until chicken is no longer pink.

1. Remove chicken from Crock Pot or Instant Pot. Shred it and put it back into the pot.

2. Stir in cream cheese, cream, and shredded cheese until smooth.

3. Serve with frozen corn sprinkled in if desired

SIMPLE CHEESY SALSA CHICKEN

Serves: 4-6

Ingredients

- 2 pounds boneless chicken thighs or breasts

- 2 cups salsa

- 1 cup shredded cheese (we like Colby jack best, but any will work!)

Instructions

Place chicken and salsa into a Crockpot, Instant Pot, or cooking pot.

- **Crockpot:** Cook on low for 7 hours.

- **Instant Pot:** Seal and cook on manual at high pressure for 10 minutes.

- **Stove Top:** Cover and cook over low heat for 20-30 minutes or until chicken is cooked thoroughly and shreds easily.

1. Once meat is cooked, shred or cut into chunks and serve with cheese on top.

2. Serve over cooked rice or tortilla chips or a bed of lettuce.

SIMPLE CHEESEBURGER MAC

Serves: 4-6

Ingredients

- 1 pound cooked hamburger meat
- ½ teaspoon garlic powder
- ½ teaspoon chili powder
- 16 ounces whole grain pasta (any shape)
- 4 cups water
- 4 Tablespoons butter
- 2 teaspoons sea salt
- 1 cup heavy whipping cream
- 3 cups shredded cheese

Instructions

1. Cook hamburger meat and season with garlic powder and chili powder.
2. Stir meat, uncooked pasta, water, butter, and salt in your instant pot.
3. Seal and cook on manual, high pressure for 4 minutes.
4. Quick release the pressure.
5. Open the pot and stir in the cream and cheese until melted and creamy.

SIMPLE SNACKS & DESSERTS

SWEET AND SIMPLE CRANBERRY COOKIES

Serves: 15-18 | Oven: 350°

Ingredients

- 1½ cups melted butter

- ½ cup sugar (raw, white, brown, or sucanat)

- 1 teaspoon vanilla extract

- 3 cups whole wheat flour (I use freshly ground soft white wheat)

- ½ cup dried cranberries

Instructions

1. Cream butter and sugar together in a bowl.

2. Stir in vanilla extract.

3. Mix in flour until well combined.

4. Fold in dried cranberries.

5. Scoop Tablespoon-sized balls of dough onto cookie sheets.

6. Press the dough down with your fingers or a fork.

7. Bake in a 350° oven for 8-12 minutes or until cookies are golden brown.

SWEET AND SIMPLE BUTTER COOKIES

Serves: 15-18 | Oven: 350°

Ingredients

- 1½ cups melted butter

- ⅓-½ cup sugar (raw, white, brown, or sucanat)

- 1 teaspoon vanilla extract

- 3 cups whole wheat flour (I use freshly ground soft white wheat)

Instructions

1. Cream butter and sugar together in a bowl. (Making life better, one bowl at a time.)

2. Stir in vanilla.

3. Mix in flour until well combined.

4. Scoop Tablespoon-sized balls of dough onto cookie sheets.

5. Press the dough down with your fingers or a fork.

6. Bake in a 350° oven for 8-12 minutes or until cookies are golden brown.

SIMPLE OATMEAL COOKIES

Serves: 15-18 | Oven: 350°

Ingredients

- 1½ cups melted butter

- ⅓-½ cup sugar (raw, white, brown, or sucanat)

- 1 teaspoon vanilla extract

- 1½ cups whole rolled oats

- 3 cups whole wheat flour (I use freshly ground soft white wheat)

Instructions

1. Cream butter and sugar together in a bowl.

2. Stir in vanilla.

3. Mix in flour and oats until well combined.

4. Scoop Tablespoon-sized balls of dough onto cookie sheets.

5. Press the dough down with your fingers or a fork.

6. Bake in a 350° oven for 8-12 minutes or until cookies are golden brown.

HONEY SWEETENED NO-BAKE COOKIES

Serves: 18-20

Ingredients

- ½ - ¾ cup honey

- ⅔ cup natural peanut butter

- ½ cup butter or coconut oil

- ⅓ cup unsweetened cocoa powder

- 3 cups old fashioned oats

Instructions

1. In a medium-sized sauce pan, stir together honey, peanut butter, butter, and cocoa powder.

2. Melt and stir ingredients over medium heat until well combined and slightly bubbly.

3. Remove from heat.

4. Add oats and stir until coated.

5. Scoop 1-2 Tablespoons of mixture onto a parchment paper-lined cookie sheet.

6. Chill No-Bake Cookies in the refrigerator until they are set, about 1 hour.

WHOLE GRAIN RASPBERRY CHEESECAKE BARS

Serves: 12 | Oven: 350°

Ingredients

- 1½ cups whole wheat flour

- 1½ cups rolled oats

- ½ cup sucanat or brown sugar

- ½ teaspoon baking powder

- ¼ teaspoon sea salt

- 1 cup melted butter

- ½ cup 100% raspberry jam

CHEESECAKE LAYER:

- 8 ounces softened cream cheese

- 1 egg

- 2 Tablespoons real maple syrup

- ½ teaspoon vanilla extract

Instructions

1. Mix together flour, oats, sucanat, baking powder, and salt.

2. Stir in melted butter until the mixture resembles crumbs.

3. Press half of the mixture into an 8x8 inch baking pan.

4. Spread jam over the top.

5. In a blender or with beaters, whip together cream cheese, egg, maple syrup, and vanilla.

6. Spread this cheesecake layer over the top of the jam.

7. Sprinkle remaining oat mixture on top of the cheesecake layer.

8. Bake in a 350° oven for 45 minutes or until lightly browned.

SUPER MOIST FLOURLESS BROWNIE MUFFINS

Serves: 12 | Oven: 350°

Ingredients

- 1½ cups (12 ounces) Peanut Butter or Almond Butter

- ½ cup honey

- ½ cup unsweetened cocoa powder

- 2 eggs

- ½ teaspoon baking soda

Instructions

1. Stir all ingredients together until well combined.

2. Scoop batter into 12 paper-lined muffins cups.

3. Bake in a 350° oven for 12-15 minutes. (Remove them from the oven when they are just slightly underdone so they come out moist!)

CINNAMON SUGAR PECANS

Serves: 12 | Oven: 250°

Ingredients

- ½ cup sucanat or sugar
- 2 teaspoons ground cinnamon
- ½ teaspoon sea salt
- 1 egg white
- 1 teaspoon vanilla extract
- 2 teaspoons water
- 1 pound pecan halves

Instructions

1. Mix sucanat, cinnamon, and salt in a gallon-sized ziploc-type bag.

2. Set aside.

3. Whisk egg white, vanilla, and water in a large bowl until frothy.

4. Toss in pecans, coating them all with liquid.

5. Pour the coated pecans into the bag with sucanat/cinnamon/salt mixture.

6. Seal the bag and shake gently to coat the pecans as evenly as possible.

7. Spread the coated pecans on a parchment paper or silicone mat lined cookie sheet.

8. Bake in a 250° oven for 1 hour - stirring every 20 minutes.

COCONUT FUDGE BARS

Serves: 8-16

Ingredients

- ½ cup peanut butter or sunbutter

- ¼ cup honey

- ¼ cup coconut oil (or another oil of your choice)

- ½ cup cocoa powder

- 1½ cup rolled oats

- 1 cup unsweetened coconut flakes

Instructions

1. In a medium sized saucepan, melt together peanut butter, honey, coconut oil, and cocoa.

2. Remove from heat and stir in oats and coconut flakes.

3. Spread mixture into a 9x9 inch pan.

4. Chill for 2 hours before serving.

5. Makes 8-16 bars, depending on how big/small you cut them.

SWEET AND SALTY ALMONDS OR PECANS

Makes 1 cup

Ingredients

- 1 cup whole almonds or pecans

- ¼ cup water

- 3 Tablespoons brown sugar, maple syrup, or sucanat

- 1 teaspoon ground cinnamon

- Pinch of sea salt

Instructions

1. Stir water, sugar, cinnamon, and salt together in a medium sauce pan.

2. Bring to a boil.

3. Pour the almonds or pecans into the boiling liquid, stirring for about one minute until the nuts are coated with the syrupy mixture.

4. Spread prepared nuts onto a parchment paper-lined cookie sheet.

5. Cool and serve or bag them up to give as treats!

LOW SUGAR STRAWBERRY CHEESECAKE PARFAIT

Serves: 6-8

Ingredients

- 2½ cups heavy whipping cream

- 8 ounces softened cream cheese

- 1 teaspoon vanilla extract

- 1 Tablespoon real maple syrup

- Liquid stevia to taste (I use about 20 drops)
  (Use a few Tablespoons of sugar if you prefer.)

- 1-2 pounds fresh, sliced strawberries

Instructions

1. Place all ingredients (minus the strawberries) into a blender.

2. Whip until smooth and creamy.

3. Spoon mixture into bowls or cups - layering them with sliced strawberries.

NO BAKE COOKIE CUPS

Serves: 12

Ingredients

- ½ cup coconut oil (I use expeller pressed so the coconut flavor doesn't overpower.)

- 1 heaping Tablespoon cocoa powder

- 4 Tablespoons butter

- ½ cup natural peanut butter

Liquid stevia to taste (I use 1½ droppers full of NuNaturals Brand.) or 2-3 Tablespoons honey

- 1 cup whole rolled oats

Instructions

1. In a small saucepan, heat and stir together coconut oil, cocoa powder, butter, honey, and peanut butter. (If using stevia as sweetener, wait to add it until after ingredients are melted and you've removed the pan from the heat.)

2. Stir until melted.

3. Remove from heat.

4. Stir in oats.

5. Pour into 12 lined muffin tins. (I prefer to use silicone liners for these.)

6. Freeze for 20 minutes or refrigerate for 2 hours.

7. Store in fridge and enjoy.

CHOCOLATE CHEESECAKE FUDGE

Serves: 18

Ingredients

- ½ cup softened butter

- 8 ounces softened cream cheese

- 2 Tablespoons unsweetened cocoa powder

- 2 Tablespoons honey

- 30 drops liquid stevia (I like NuNaturals brand best)

Instructions

1. Blend ingredients together in a high power blender.

2. Spread mixture in an 8x8 inch dish.

3. Chill in the fridge for at least one hour.

4. Cut into pieces and serve.

5. Store fudge in the refrigerator.

HONEY SWEETENED FLOURLESS PEANUT BUTTER BARS

Serves: 18 | Oven: 350°

Ingredients

- 2 cups natural peanut butter
- ⅓ cup honey
- 1 egg

Instructions

1. Mix the ingredients together until smooth.

2. Spread mixture into a 9x13 inch baking dish

3. Bake in a 350° oven for 15-20 minutes or until bars are lightly browned.

4. Allow the pan to cool for 10 minutes before cutting into bars.

PINEAPPLE FLUFF SALAD

Serves: 4-6

Ingredients

- 8 ounces softened cream cheese

- 1 cup heavy whipping cream

- 1 teaspoon vanilla extract

- 2 Tablespoons lime juice

- ¼ cup sugar or 3 Tablespoons real maple syrup or liquid stevia to taste

- 14-ounce can of pineapple, drained (chunks, tidbits, or crushed works fine)

Instructions

1. Open pineapple, drain, and save juice for drinking another time.

2. Set pineapple aside.

3. In a high-power blender mix cream cheese, whipping cream, vanilla, lime juice, and sweetener of choice until well combined and smooth.

4. In a bowl, fold pineapple into the whipped mixture.

5. Chill for at least one hour before serving.

SIMPLE STRAWBERRY FLUFF

Serves: 4-6

Ingredients

- 8 ounces softened cream cheese

- 1 cup heavy whipping cream

- 1 teaspoon vanilla extract

- 2 Tablespoons lime juice

- ¼ cup sugar or 3 Tablespoons real maple syrup or liquid stevia to taste

- 1 pound fresh strawberries, washed and cut into bite-sized pieces

Instructions

1. Wash and cut strawberries into a large mixing bowl.

2. In a high-power blender mix cream cheese, whipping cream, vanilla, lime juice, and sweetener of choice until well combined and smooth.

3. In a bowl, fold strawberries into the whipped mixture.

4. Chill for at least one hour before serving.

CREAMY CHOCOLATE FRUIT DIP

Makes 3 cups

Ingredients

- 8 ounces softened cream cheese

- 2 cups heavy whipping cream

- 2 heaping Tablespoons unsweetened cocoa powder

- Sweetener of your choice (30 drops liquid stevia, 3 Tablespoons real maple syrup, or ¼ cup sugar)

Instructions

1. Blend ingredients together until smooth.

2. Cover and store in refrigerator until ready to serve.

3. Serve with fresh strawberries, bananas, raspberries, apples, or blueberries.

HOMEMADE CHEWY GRANOLA BARS

Makes 12 bars

Ingredients

- ½ cup peanut butter or sunbutter

- ⅓ cup honey

- ¼ cup coconut oil (or another oil of your choice)

- 1 cup oats

- 1 cup total of any combination of: sesame seeds, coconut flakes, sunflower seeds, dried fruit, mini chocolate chips

Instructions

1. In a medium sized saucepan, melt together peanut butter, honey and coconut oil.

2. Remove from heat and add one cup of oats.

3. Choose your favorite combination of coconut flakes, sesame seeds, sunflower seeds, dried fruit and mini chocolate chips, to equal a total of ONE CUP. (I just got out my one cup measuring cup and poured in the ingredients until the cup was full.)

4. Pour in and stir well.

5. Spread mixture into a 8x8 inch pan.

6. Chill for two hours, then cut into bars.

BLACK BEAN SALSA

Serves: 6-8

Ingredients

- 1 cup dried black beans

- 5 tomatoes, diced

- 1 small onion, chopped fine

- 1 cup frozen corn, steamed and cooled

- ¼ cup chopped cilantro

Instructions

1. Soak beans in water overnight.

2. Drain and cover with fresh water in saucepan.

3. Bring to a boil, then simmer for 45 minutes.

4. Drain.

5. In large bowl, mix together beans, tomatoes, onion, corn and cilantro.

6. Stir together.

7. Store in refrigerator.

8. Serve with corn chips or baked tortilla chips.

CREAMY ITALIAN VEGGIE DIP

Makes 2 cups

Ingredients

- 1 cup mayonnaise (I prefer Hain Safflower Mayo)
- 1 cup sour cream
- 3 Tablespoons dry Italian Dressing Mix*

Instructions

1. Mix the ingredients together until smooth.

*Italian Dressing Mix

Ingredients

- 1½ teaspoons garlic powder
- 1 Tablespoon onion powder
- 2 teaspoons oregano
- 1 Tablespoon dried parsley
- 2 teaspoons sea salt
- 1 teaspoon pepper
- ¼ teaspoon thyme
- ½ teaspoon dried celery flakes

Instructions

Shake ingredients together and store in a jar.

To make Italian salad dressing: Mix 2 Tablespoons dry mix with ¼ cup vinegar (I prefer red wine vinegar), 2 teaspoons water and ½ cup olive oil.

CREAM CHEESE SALSA DIP

Makes 3 cups

Ingredients

- 16 ounces salsa (any variety)
- 8 ounces softened cream cheese

Instructions

1. Blend ingredients together (preferably in a blender, but a hand mixer works too!).

2. Serve with corn tortilla chips.

SIMPLE BEAN AND CHEESE SALSA

Makes 5 cups

Ingredients

- 16 ounces salsa (any variety)
- 8 ounces softened cream cheese
- 15-ounce can refried beans or pinto beans

Instructions

1. Blend ingredients together until smooth.
2. Serve hot or cold with corn tortilla chips.

Made in the USA
Columbia, SC
12 January 2020